Cards, Toasts & Notes For the Office
Express Yourself in Rhyme

Marcia Goldlist

Dedication

This book is dedicated to all those who would like to make the office more relaxed and fun!

TABLE OF CONTENTS

Introduction

We all know that the office is not always fun
But there is no reason that this cannot be somewhat undone.
You can make your office more pleasant
Without even buying a present.
Just write notes once in a while
And see someone in your office smile.
Write a rhyme to announce a meeting
Or for after a holiday to send a welcome back greeting.
If in your office you would like to improve the mood
Don't just sit around and brood,
Find an appropriate rhyme
And you will see that things will improve in a short time!
.

Birthday Wishes

~Birthday -1

Today is your day, so with you everyone should agree,
But not everything in this world is as it should be.
However, your work and your gentle way,
Has never led us astray.
With a polite manner you help things get done,
Yet you also remember that it is important to have fun.
We all wish you a healthy year,
With lots of good wishes which are sincere.

~Birthday -2

We want to celebrate your birthday
In a special way
So we would like to invite you to lunch
Where we can talk and munch.
I'm sure that you know that the table will be set in a lovely display,
And the food will be as good as any café!
Are you willing to share with *Sue your special day?
As her birthday from yours is not far away,
For **Monday, April 21st this invitation is set.
So don't forget!
We can't wait to celebrate with you both in a special way,
Although we also hope that you will make a birthday wish today!!!

*Fill in other worker's name.
**Fill in proper day and date.

~Birthday -3

It's your birthday
So from your desk we want to take you away.
Please come for lunch with us
So over you we can make a little fuss.

~Birthday -4

Working here we cannot promise you wealth,
But we can hope for you good health.
We are all wishing you a happy birthday
Hoping many good things come your way.

~Birthday -5

At *ten o'clock we want you to take a little break
So that we can celebrate your birthday with some cake.
We are all wishing you a great year,
With lots of things that will bring you good cheer.

*Can change the time.

~Birthday -6

We hope that you leave work early today
To celebrate your birthday in some special way.
Go out for dinner,
Or just open a bottle of wine that is a winner.
It doesn't matter much as long as some celebration you create
Because for your birthday we want you in a joyous state.

~Birthday -7

At *2:30 we will all shirk
Our work
To wish you a happy birthday
In the proper way.
So 'till then don't be blue,
We are all thinking of you!

*Fill in the correct time.

~Birthday -8

Today
Is your birthday
And we all want to shout,
"Run! Get out!"
But we know that you wouldn't leave
So, what would it achieve?
To your desk you would cleave
As in hard work you believe.
Stop choking!
Just joking!
We will try to make sure that you have a great day
So that tonight you will be in the mood to go out and play!

Coming Back To Work After An Absence

~Coming Back -1

It is great to have you back.
Without you we did feel a lack.
We missed you,
Talking and hearing your point of view.
You were definitely not forgot
And it is great having you back in your spot!

~Coming Back -2

To you we want to give a great big "hello",
Especially because the amount of work in this office is about to
grow.
We hope that you missed us at least a bit,
And simply that we're glad you're back we want to transmit.

Corporate Sponsor

As a corporate sponsor we consider you a truly special friend,
So to you an extra thank you we would like to extend.
Thanks to corporations like yours this world is a better place,
And we can see on more *children a smile on their face.

*Can change this to anything appropriate.

Customer Response

~Customer Response -1

To us you did not come back,
And we would really like to know what we did lack.
Value your comments we do,
Your advice we would like to pursue.
Please let us know why you did not return,
From your comments we would really like to learn.

~Customer Response -2

We would really like to know
If with you our service did rank high or low.
It is important to know what you feel
So that we can steadily improve until we are ideal!
Thanks for your time in filling out this questionnaire.
You can be sure that we will read it with care!

~Customer Response -3

We would like to know what we did wrong and what we did right
Because for your loyalty we are willing to fight!
Please fill out the form below
So how to improve we will know!

Employee Of The Year

What does it mean to be the employee of the year?
It means that someone's work we especially revere.
He or she has worked especially hard.
Often to personal time giving no regard.
Helping others with a smile.
Making you feel that every question and statement is worthwhile.
Work is done with special care,
And it is done with flair!
When I call this year's appointee,
Will he or she please stand up and stand beside me.

Voting for Employee of the Year

Please vote on who you think should be the employee of the year.
Someone who to their work has been very sincere.
It should be someone that you think has given their all
And upon whom for help you thought you could freely call.
Please hand in your vote in the coming days
For who you think deserves our praise.

Get Well

~Get Well -1

We would like to let you know of our concern,
And our wish that with full strength to work you will return.

~Get Well -2

Welcome to the meeting,
You deserve a special greeting!
We know that you have been rather sick
And yet to come today you gave yourself a little kick.
We think that it is great that you are always so upbeat,
We wish you a recovery that is truly complete!

Giving A Pin

Here is a pin that we hope you will wear with pride,
As you scatter worldwide.
We know that you have worked very hard,
And for all of your work we hold you in high regard.

Improvement

Feel free
To write a note to me.
It can be long or short,
About something that you disagree with or support.
Thanks for taking the time
For helping to make our work place more sublime.

Kitchen Area

Dirty Dishes in the Sink

~Dirty Dishes in the Sink -1

There were dirty dishes in the sink
And they were starting to stink.
Please wash your dishes right away
So that any food left on them does not have time to decay.

~Dirty Dishes in the Sink -2

Dirty dishes sitting around.
Oh what germs can be found!
This is a sight I rather not see.
Don't you agree?
Please keep the place clean,
So we don't need a vaccine!

Missing Food from Fridge

~Missing Food from Fridge -1

Beware! This fridge ate my food
And I think that it is very rude.
I'm warning you in advance,
You may not want to take a chance.
Keep your food and drinks far away
Or you too could be left in dismay!

~Missing Food from Fridge -2

Warning!
I could not find my food this morning.
Perhaps you saw it run away?
You called "stop" but it would not stay?
If this fridge is not acting nicely to the food,
If it is in any way being rude,
Please inform me right away,
So that I can take care of it without delay.

Using Boiling Water

If the boiling water in the kettle you finish,
Or for less than a cup it did diminish,
Please fill the kettle and turn it on once more,
As I keep filling the kettle and coming back to find that there is no
water left to pour.
Thank you for helping with this deed
So that to have a hot drink I too can succeed!

Leaving Work

~Leaving Work -1

Your time has come to go,
About this we are sad, we hope you know.
It's been lots of fun working with you,
There is no one else that we would have preferred on our crew.
We hope that more of you we will see,
Because to be with you is as pleasant as can be.
This present is a little token,
Hoping that all thoughts of us will not be broken.

~Leaving Work -2

We hope that at the hour of ten,
You will be ready to put down your pen.
We want to say our goodbyes
And give you a little surprise.

~Leaving Work -3

At *2:00 in your honor we are serving something to eat,
As sitting around eating and talking on your last day just can't be
beat.

*Write in the time.

~Leaving Work -4

So, today working at *the food bank is your last day,
And we will surely miss you when you are far away.
We are sure that many interesting things you will see,
But that we will miss you, we all agree.
For us you have helped to make things run smoothly without any
doubt,
But that is not what made you stand out.
Your personality, friendliness and humor,
Are far more than a rumor.
We always saw you with a smile,
And talking with you was always worthwhile.
We are truly sorry to see you go,
But we are sure with so many new experiences in **Chicago your
face will be aglow.
So be healthy,
And don't worry whether or not you are wealthy.
Enjoy yourself a lot,
But remember the rules that to you your mother taught.
Don't commit any crime,
And remember us from time to time.
We would love to receive an email from you,
To tell us of various experiences you did accrue.
We must say bye for now,
And we hope that **Chicago to you will be one big WOW!

*Fill in name of company.
**Fill in name of new place of work, or new city.

~Leaving Work -5

*You have been **Jill's loyal aide,
But more than that, true friendship have you displayed.
You have always given good advice,
But above all you are simply really nice.
It is sad that you are leaving the ***food bank team,
Your work really has been supreme.
We are relieved that at least we will see you now and then.
What would we ever do if we would not see you again?
With our wish please comply,
And every once in a while come by.

*If this is not relevant leave out the first two lines.
**Write in name of superior.
***Write in the name of the company, project or division.

~Leaving Work -6

We will miss hearing you talk to yourself.
We will miss wondering if beside you is a little elf.
We will miss your laughter.
But we will definitely remember you forever after.
We don't know what we will do without you.
Perhaps before you go you can give us a clue.

~Leaving Work -7

This plant is for you,
We really think that it is due.
We know that you didn't want anything when you went today,
But this is just a little something for you to take away.
It really was nice working with you,
And we hope that this is not *adieu*.

~Leaving Work -8

You certainly helped *the hospital gift shop along,
You helped it to become strong.
**We hope that you will have good memories of all the years,
That you have worked with not only our office, but the
customers, and the volunteers.
Well, your time has come for a whole new beginning,
And with this decision we hope that you are grinning.
There's so much that you can do now.
You can take up a new sport, or pottery, or learn to milk a cow.
With your family you can spend more time.
You can walk in nature and other things which can be sublime.
We truly wish you well in all that you decide to do,
Whether it is something you have never tried or something that
you renew.
The most important thing is to take care of yourself,
And to listen to within you to the little elf.
We all wish you the best,
In whatever your quest.

*Write in name of company or project.
**You can leave out this line and the next if not relevant.

~Leaving Work -9

So, the time has come for you to leave,
And over this we do grieve.
We weren't sure what to make you for this little brunch,
As we understand that you have very specific ideas about what
you like to munch.
We hope that this brunch meets with your approval,
And that you know that your condemnation of the cafeteria food
has nothing to do with your removal.
You will certainly be missed.
Your stories and laughter have been hard to resist.
We will really miss every morning your little story,
Of battling traffic and finding a parking spot which seem to bring
you glory.
We wish you lots of luck finding a new career,
And if you don't succeed perhaps here you will reappear.
So, the time has come to say goodbye.
We hope that to come by and say hello you won't be shy.
We wish you luck in whatever you do,
And that you find something worthwhile to pursue.

~Leaving Work -10

We are very sorry to see you go,
It was nice to have you here though.
You *weren't here that long,
But you helped to make our team strong.
It was great to get to know you better,
We hope that from time to time you will drop us an email letter.
On your new job we would like to offer you congratulations.
We hope that you fit in without any complications.
Of course the crew can't be as nice as us,
But not everything in a job can be a plus.
**We are really going to miss your curiosity,
And hope that you are not leaving with any animosity.
**With you leaving we are not sure how we will keep track of
what is going on,
For in this endeavor you were an important pawn.
We sincerely wish you all the best,
And until you begin your new job enjoy the rest!

*Can change it to, "You were here for long,
And you helped make our team strong."
**If not appropriate leave this line and the following
corresponding line out.

~Leaving Work –11

It has really been a pleasure to work with you,
You really became an integral part of our crew,
Not at all like you were just passing through.

You were really put to the test,
With you we really were impressed,
And we all agree that you now deserve a rest.

We wish you happiness in whatever you pursue,
And hope that every once in a while you'll pass through,
As your friendship we want to pursue.

~Leaving Work -12

Your time with us was short,
But you really did add a lot of support.
You entered lots of data quickly and well,
And you even *made many friends before it was time to say
farewell.
We understand that now it is time for you to move on,
But of course we wanted to say a proper goodbye before you were
gone.
This **breakfast is a little thank you from us all,
For your work and your input about ***medicine, food and
anything else that did bounce off the wall.
Of course we wish you all the best,
And may you have success in your life's quest.

*Write in anything appropriate.
**Can substitute lunch or gift.
***You can change topics listed.

~Leaving Work -13

It has been very nice having you work with us.
You have done a good job and haven't made any fuss.
You are very pleasant to have around.
We wish for your blessings to abound.
Unfortunately we can't keep you working here,
But we hope that better things for you on your horizon will
appear.

~Leaving Work -14

We're not too sure what you thought,
Before in this job you were caught.
You were always calm, cool and collected,
And for this and your work you have become well respected.
You really will be missed,
And we hope that offers come your way that you cannot resist.

~Leaving Work -15

To *Jill we will say farewell,
Even though **she has been swell.
For the time we had together we will have a little celebration.
We will meet you in the usual location.

*Fill in name of worker.
**Can be changed to "he".

~Leaving Work –16

We are so sorry that you are leaving our little team,
Working with you has been supreme.
We certainly wish you all the best,
And hope that you find health, happiness and fulfillment in your
quest.

For an Intern or Volunteer

~Intern or Volunteer -1

You have been just great!
Over this there can be no debate.
You always had a smile,
And your work was more than worthwhile.
You helped us with *media, mailings and more,
And you never acted like any of it was a chore.
We wish you all the best in whatever you decide to pursue.
To you we want to say one big thank you.

*You can change the jobs to anything appropriate.

~Intern or Volunteer -2

You helped us get out the packets with success,
And you did it all without feeling any stress!
We appreciate your folding, and preparing the packets for mail
And that you checked the letters paying attention to detail.
We wish you the best with whatever you decide to pursue,
And once again, we would like to thank you.

~Intern or Volunteer -3

It is hard to believe
That you are going to leave.
We were really pleased with your work.
Having you here for us was really a perk.

Leaving Work Temporarily

~Leaving Temporarily -1

We are sure that the *chicken here you will not really miss,
But if we didn't tell you how much we will miss you, we would really be amiss.
You are always so cheery when you walk in,
No matter how badly the traffic got under your skin.
We really hope that only a small break this parting will be.
That you are very easy to work with we all agree.

*Write in something appropriate (lunches, some aspect of work, coffee, etc.)

~Leaving Temporarily -2

We hope that your time off will be just great,
And that you will keep us up-to-date.
We look forward to seeing you back,
As with your work you have quite a knack.

Lost Articles

~Lost Articles -1

It is just not fair,
I put my *cup down with care
And now it is not there.
And I don't even have a spare!
Oh, I am in such despair!!
I can't imagine that it vanished into thin air.
If you know anything about this affair
Perhaps with me this information you could share,
Or just replace it when I am unaware –
If not – take care!!
And beware!

*Fill in any article that goes missing such as a pen, stapler, etc.

~Lost Articles -2

My *mug is nowhere to be found
And I have looked all around.
If my *cup you did take
I'm sure that it was by mistake.
I would appreciate you bringing it back
Before I have a panic attack!

*Fill in any article that goes missing such as a pen, stapler, etc.

Meeting

~Meeting -1

At *2:30, in our regular spot, we will be having our meeting
And for you there will be seating.
Please come with your ideas and open mind
So that to any problems solutions we can find.

*Fill in appropriate time.

~Meeting -2

Your attendance is requested
So that we can go over some ideas that were suggested.
About these we would like to talk,
So please let me know if you can come on *April, 21st at ten
o'clock.
In my office we will meet,
To see if we can make some suggestions concrete.

*Fill in appropriate date and time.

~Meeting -3

I would like to have a meeting
And you are one of the people that I would like to be greeting.
So please let me know if at *13:30 on Monday, April 21st you can
come
So I know if for this meeting there will be a large enough sum.

*Fill in appropriate time, day and date.

~Meeting -4

I think that things are going along great
But it is time for an update.
Tomorrow let's get together and talk
In my office at *eleven o'clock.

*Fill in appropriate time.

~Meeting -5

A reminder to you I want to convey
That we have a meeting in the board room at *10:30 today.
Please do not be late
As we have a lot that we need to update.

*Fill in appropriate time.

~Meeting -6

Today, in *the staff room we will meet
Where from **3:00-4:30 our work we will complete.
Come and make your coffee or tea
And let's see on what we can agree.

*Fill in appropriate location.
**Fill in appropriate times.

New Year Wishes

~New Year -1

Happy Holidays to the whole staff
On the management's behalf.
Take a break, even if your work is not done.
Party and have fun!
For the new year we are wishing you all the best
Hoping that with good fortune you and your family will be
blessed!

~New Year -2

Wishing you and your family a healthy new year
Full of lots of company profits which are clear.
Thank you all for your hard work.
We are very glad that this you do not shirk.
Our profits are very important to us
So we are glad that over the amount of work that you have you do
not fuss.
Without all of you the work would not get done
And I would not be able to have fun.
Seriously I give many thanks
To everyone through the ranks.
Your work is top notch
And I hardly need my scotch.
I can really rely on all of you
Your work is professional through and through.
Let's toast a new year full of smiles
And not too many trials,
Where profits are high,
And everyone is happy with their share of the pie!

Phone Memo

I want you to know
The information below:
At _____ o'clock
_____ phoned to talk.

Photocopy Machine

~Photocopy Machine -1

If your paper should become stuck,
Please don't play with the machine hoping for some luck.
Call me
And I will get it free.

~Photocopy Machine -2

If this machine has no more ink,
Or a light does blink,
Please give me a call
And I will come down the hall.
Please don't try to fix the machine
As it may not be something routine.
I would hate for you to make things worse
As then upon you I may put a curse!

Private Phone Calls

~Private Phone Calls -1

If in the office you insist on having a private conversation
Please make it of a short duration.
Other people are trying to get their work done
And find it hard when having to listen in to see if you are having any fun!

~Private Phone Calls -2

Please keep your voice down while you are on the phone
As in this room you are not alone.
It is hard for others to keep their concentration
While you are having a conversation.

Receiving A Bonus

Thank you for the bonus.
I know on you was the onus.
Appreciated is the work, it is nice to know,
Now forward to next *year we can go.
It is nice working with you,
Let's hope that this year goes smoothly for the whole crew.

*Can change to the next project.

Speaking One's Mind

Congratulations to you.
You saw an opening and the opportunity you did pursue.
We all think that you did the right thing,
And hope that results it does bring.
But no matter what, it laid our feelings on the table,
And we thank you for speaking up in a way that was so able.

Travel

Good Trip

~Good Trip -1

We are sure that you will have a great trip,
But we do want to give you one tip.
About all of us and the office just forget,
This is one trip that for sure you will not regret!

~Good Trip -2

From work you may only be taking off one day,
But we are so glad that you are getting away.
You're sure to feel more refreshed when you come back,
And we'll be glad to hear about your weekend over a snack.

~Good Trip -3

It is hard to write you another rhyme,
As you keep leaving us all the time.
But we do wish you a good trip, as always we do,
We can't wait to hear your stories, and your pictures to view.
We'll try to keep the office going,
Though without you it is hard to keep things flowing.
You will really be missed,
We enjoy having you in our midst.

~Good Trip -4

So, you are flying off once again.
We know by now that from traveling you cannot refrain.
We hope that some new things you will see.
That we will miss you we can almost guarantee.
Enjoy your time away from work.
We know that at times we can drive you a little berserk.

~Good Trip -5

Down south you and *Jill are to go.
When you come back we are sure that your skin will glow.
Have fun **snorkeling and bathing in the sun,
It is very important to have time together and have some fun.
Don't think of us at all,
"Office" is a word that you need not recall.
But we will truly think of you,
Because you are terrific – and that is true.

*Write in name of travelling partner or "your family".
**You can take out "snorkeling and" if it is not relevant.

~Good Trip -6

With your *brother we hope that you have a meaningful time,
Because not to spend time with a sibling is almost a crime.
So about the office don't give a thought,
Over new and old memories with your family we hope that your
mind is caught.

*Can change to sister.

~Good Trip -7

So, you're going on a trip to see the flowers,
And we hope that it gives you more powers.
We know that you will find nice places along the way to have a
snack,
And for sure more refreshed, you will come back.
Lots of colorful pictures we know that you will take,
And we look forward to seeing them while taking a break.
Of course we will miss talking to you,
But we are happy knowing that the important things in life you do
pursue.
Like being with your husband, and looking at each flower,
And of course eating sandwiches every hour.

Welcome Back

~Welcome Back -1

We are so glad to have you back,
While you were away we really did feel a lack.
Although we do have to say,
Little by little we have learned to do your job in almost every way.
But we don't think that you have to worry,
As on a few things we are still a bit blurry.
And we intend to keep it that way for a bit,
So no matter how much you enjoyed your vacation, don't even
think to quit!!!!!!!!!!!

~Welcome Back -2

We missed you while you were away,
And we actually did work, not too much did we play.
Your "Good morning" we did miss,
But we sure do hope that during the whole trip you were in a state
of bliss.
While, now you are back,
So your emails you better attack!

~Welcome Back -3

It is so nice to have you back,
Without you we almost had a panic attack.
Of course we're just joking and we're glad for you,
We know that time with your family was overdue.
We can't wait to see pictures and hear your tales,
We really are interested in all of the details.
Unfortunately for you, to get back to work it is time,
And for me it is time to end this rhyme.

~Welcome Back -4

Welcome back to work,
I'm sure that you will find that our work we did not shirk.

~Welcome Back -5

Welcome back from your time off,
We trust that no one came down with a cough.
We hope that you had good quality time with your in-laws,
And that with *Jill they didn't find many flaws.
Hopefully any thoughts of the office were far from your head,
That you just relaxed and had a good time instead.

*Fill in appropriate name.

~Welcome Back -6

It's so nice to have you back in your seat,
We sure hope that your trip could not be beat.
Pictures we hope that you have plenty to show,
And stories of how your grandchildren did grow.
Of course about the *architecture we also want to hear,
And we hope that you will be glad to know that your job did not
disappear.

*Write in anything relevant (museums, sites, food, etc.)

~Welcome Back -7

We understand that your time was swell,
And you must have lots to tell.
We're sure that you know that it was right to take a break.
You can tell us about it over some coffee and cake.

~Welcome Back -8

(This poem may not be appropriate to give to your boss but it can lighten the mood among your co-workers.)

It was so nice when you were away,
We were free and it was easy to play.
Also it was quieter we must say,
But through the email you made sure from our work we did not too much stray.
It was nice not to always feel under attack,
However, I guess we have to welcome you back.

~Welcome Back -9

We know that this trip was not all fun,
But we hope that you feel that it was worthwhile now that it is done.
We did miss you here.
Without you it did seem a bit queer.
We hope that you enjoyed the sunshine,
And that for us too much you did not pine.
Of you we were concerned,
But now you have returned.
Now that you are back,
I guess your work you better attack!!

~Welcome Back -10

Welcome back from your trip abroad,
We are sure that everyone you met was awed.
We understand that for *fundraising you two have quite a knack,
We are sure that on your trip you had good feedback.
We're sure that you were quite a smash,
We hope that your efforts bring in a lot of cash.

*May substitute getting customers, selling, etc.

~Welcome Back -11

From the virtual world we welcome you back.
We hope that returning to reality does not give you a panic attack.
We hope that being here has some perk,
But either way get back to work!!

~Welcome Back -12

You were certainly missed around here,
We kept hoping that you would just reappear.
But for good things we are told you have to wait,
So we waited and waited and finally today reappears our soul
mate.
We're so glad that you're back,
Especially because we had to pick up your slack.
We were glad to get emails and know that things were going well,
But now we can't wait to hear the stories that you have to tell.

~Welcome Back -13

We hope that while you were away of good times you did partake,
And that you had a good break.
A lot has happened while you were away,
But at least things are not in disarray.

~Welcome Back -14

You keep going away and coming back.
Does this mean that without us you feel a little lack?
Really it is nice having you back in your chair,
Even though we know that you get up wondering here and there.
But, we can't wait to hear about your trip,
And of course your pictures we do not want to skip.
So settle in for at least a few weeks,
Before you go traipsing off to more valleys or peaks.

~Welcome Back -15

I certainly hope that you had fun,
This was certainly a great way for the New Year to have begun.
Hopefully you had a special time,
And you understand I have a lot of work so you're getting a short
rhyme.

Wedding Card

~Wedding Card -1

From the *food bank staff where **Jill does work,
***Bill, we can tell you that having **Jill as a ****mother-in-law is
really a perk.
To the two of you we wish a very happy life,
Together in health and fulfillment as husband and wife.

*Fill in name of company or project.
**Fill in name of worker.
***Fill in name of bride or groom marrying into the family.
****Can change to father-in-law, sister-in-law, brother-in-law, etc.

~Wedding Card -2

May your marriage be blessed.
May you help each other through life's quest.
And in whatever you each endeavor
The important thing is to remain best friends forever!

~Wedding Card -3

Bill's office staff wishes you both all the best
And pray that your marriage will be blessed.
May you both be healthy
And realize that there are more important things than being
wealthy.

May you keep the special glow
That upon you both at your wedding did show
And together may your happiness only grow.

Welcome Back After Maternity Leave

~Maternity Leave -1

Welcome back!
We hope that it won't be too hard for you to get back on track.
May you easily get your work done,
So that you can go home to your son!
We know of *Billy you are probably thinking,
But don't worry, his bottle he is probably happily drinking.
We're sure that this year will be for you very sweet,
As you watch *Billy crawl and gradually stand on his feet.
May you and your family have a healthy year,
With many exciting firsts to cheer!

*Write in name of baby.

~Maternity Leave -2

We're sure that you still want to stay home and cuddle your little
one,
But we're glad to have you back as work still has to get done.
It was hard without you when you were away,
So we're really glad that you came back today.

~Maternity Leave -3

It's great to see you back in your chair.
And I'm glad that you found good child care.
Let's sit down at *10:00 today
And I'll fill you in on what has been going on while you were
away.

*You may change the time.

Welcoming Someone to Work

~Welcome -1

Welcome to our team.
We are sure that you will be supreme.
It will be, we are sure, pleasant having you around,
We are always here to help, so you don't have to feel weighed
down.

~Welcome -2

Welcome to the *community center team.
You are already starting to fit in it does seem.
Know that questions you don't have to suppress,
And that we wish you much success.
We hope you will like working with us.
We're sure that to the team you will be a big plus.

*Write in name of company or project.

~Welcome -3

We really like that you will now be part of the staff.
We feel good that with you we can laugh.

~Welcome -4

To the *computer team we would like to welcome you.
We hear that you are the one to take *the division to heights that
are new.
For your projects we wish much success.
We are sure that us you will impress.

*Write the name of the company, project, or department.

~Welcome -5

To this job we would like to welcome you,
We are happy to share the knowledge that we did accrue,
And we are sure that you will be adding a new idea, or two.

We look forward to see how the *department will grow,
We're sure that your ideas will shortly begin to show,
Before long you will be leading us away from the status quo.

We wish you much success,
We hope that you will not be under too much stress,
And that your ideas get us into the press.

*Can substitute project, company, etc.

~Welcome –6

Welcome to our team,
You will help make come true our dream.
Lots of money should touch your hands,
As our work does expand to many lands.
We hope that you understand that your work in this place,
Helps put a smile on many a face.

~Welcome –7

Welcome to the team.
From what we've heard you will be supreme.
May you have an easy transition
Into your new position.
If you need help with any task,
To any of us feel free to ask.
We hope that you find this job to be ideal.
And may you have the strength to tackle it with zeal.

~Welcome –8

An official welcome we would like to send to you.
A good working relationship we certainly expect to pursue.
Any question you can ask us without hesitation,
Whether about a report, an email or a *donation.
Thank goodness for telephone calls and emails,
We're sure that we will always be able to work out any details.
We're sure that we will get along just fine,
**It's just too bad that we can't sit down over a glass of wine.

*Can change to foundation, location, rotation, corporation, computation.
**Can change to "Now let's make arrangements to sit down over a glass of wine."

Wishing Someone Well in Their New Job

In a new job you are about to get started,
And we're sure that you will do it full hearted.
*We will really miss you here at home,
But we know that you also need time to roam.
We are sure that you will do a good job,
And not just sit around like a blob.
Your co-workers will benefit from your work,
And we hope that you feel a perk.
In your new job we wish you good luck,
And hope that you make a decent buck.

*Take out this line and the next if not appropriate.

About The Author

Marcia Goldlist was born in Toronto, Canada. She has a Masters of Education from the University of Toronto. In 2000 she moved to Israel with her husband and 4 daughters. She is currently the mother-in-law to three and happy grandmother to three adorable grandsons!

Marcia began by writing in rhyme for family events. She has written for special occasions such as the engagements and weddings of her daughters and the birth of a grandson when her rhymes were read in front of guests. At work Marcia started writing rhymes for staff birthdays, office memos, to disseminate information, to welcome new staff and to say goodbye to the old. As a result of this she was asked to write for other people's personal and family occasions.

The compliments and encouragement that Marcia received encouraged her to put her poetry into books so that others could also make special occasions fun and meaningful.

More rhyming books by Marcia Goldlist:
~Birthday Cards & Toasts:
  Express Yourself in Rhyme.
~Cards & Toasts For Almost All Occasions:
  Express Yourself in Rhyme
~Enjoying Genesis: The Bible in Rhyme

If you enjoyed this book look for Marcia's upcoming book:
~Enjoying Exodus: The Bible in Rhyme

Visit Marcia's blog Enjoying the Bible Online for discussion points and projects related to the Bible. You can visit the blog at: http://enjoyingthebible.wordpress.com.

www.ingramcontent.com/pod-product-compliance
Lightning Source LLC
Chambersburg PA
CBHW030543290526
45786CB00004B/1848